DENVER, COLORADO

A PHOTOGRAPHIC PORTRAIT

PHOTOGRAPHY BY

John Kieffer

First published in the United States
of America by:

Twin Lights Publishers, Inc.
8 Hale Street
Rockport, Massachusetts 01966
Telephone: (978) 546-7398
http://www.twinlightspub.com

ISBN: 1-885435-71-1
ISBN: 978-1-885435-71-2

10 9 8 7 6 5 4 3 2 1

Red Rocks Park *(opposite)*

The natural sandstone formations of
Red Rocks Park are 250 million years
old. Dinosaur tracks and evidence of a
giant sea serpent and flying reptiles
are found throughout this uniquely
beautiful place.

(jacket front)

Colorado State Capitol.

(jacket back)

Denver's glittering skyline at night.

Editorial researched and written by:
Francesca and Duncan Yates
www.freelancewriters.com

Book design by:
SYP Design & Production, Inc.
www.sypdesign.com

Printed in China

INTRODUCTION

There was gold in the water that day back in 1858, when a group of prospectors settled down at the confluence of Cherry Creek and the South Platte River to stake their claim in the first, heady days of the Colorado gold rush.

Hopes and dreams paved the way to Denver during its early days as a fast-growing mining town of muddy roads in a remote and sometimes cold and snowy location. With the inspiring backdrop of the Colorado Rockies, visionary city planners, led by Major Robert W. Speer, persevered to create a shining "Paris of the West." Originally established by the promise of great prosperity, Denver has remained true to her ideal, striking gold in a multitude of ways, right up to today.

The Mile-High City is the largest metropolitan area in a six-hundred-mile radius. It is the region's hub for cultural programs, financial institutions, commercial business, educational innovations, and transportation. With the largest city park system in the country and more days of sunshine than Miami Beach, Denver is one of America's most desirable regions.

The city is a center for the arts as well; its glittering Performing Arts Complex is second in size only to New York City's Lincoln Center with music, theater and dance lighting up the performance halls and dazzling audiences almost every night. In addition, Denver's wildly successful 16th Street Mall is the shining star of a bustling and exciting downtown.

Nearby, the spectacular Rocky Mountains provide year-round pleasure with incredible views that change with every season. A winter paradise for white powder skiing and snowboarding and a summer haven for hiking and rock climbing, the high country is a place to commune with nature as it sets a more quiet pace away from the busy city.

Turn the pages of this inspiring photographic portrait by Colorado photographer, John Kieffer, and indulge in the stirring images of America's Mile-High City and the regal mountains at its back door.

City Park *(opposite)*

On a clear, sunny day, Denver sparkles as one of America's most livable cities. In the foreground, Ferril Lake reflects the beauty of an historic pavilion at City Park. In the distance, the snow-capped Rockies silently reign over the spectacular landscape.

State Capitol *(top and bottom)*

The interior of the State Capitol's dome features sixteen stained glass windows. Each honors a distinguished Colorado pioneer, including, Denver's namesake, General James William Denver and Chief Ouray, of the Ute Nation's Uncompahgre Tribe.

The Pride of Denver *(opposite)*

Long before Colorado became a state and Denver became its official capital, land was optimistically set aside for the statehouse. The magnificent Greek Corinthian-style Capitol was completed in 1908, using native granite and marble, and luminous, polished brass.

The interior wall wainscoting is rare Beulah Red Marble, found nowhere else in the world except Beulah, Colorado. The gleaming Capitol dome is covered in two-hundred ounces of pure gold leaf, symbolizing the state's heritage and prosperity.

Broncho Buster at the Civic Center

In 1920, renowned Denver sculptor, Alexander Phimister Proctor, faced a major challenge while working on this magnificent bronco-riding cowboy. The male model for the statue, Slim Ridings, was jailed for horse rustling, yet Proctor was so determined to complete his statue that he put up the bail to free Ridings so he could continue the modeling job. *Broncho Buster* and *On the War Trail* are two outstanding sculptures by Proctor that can be found on the Civic Center grounds.

Civic Center Park in Bloom

Denver's grand Civic Center Park is known nationally for its distinctive, symmetrical, Neoclassical design of formal gardens, fountains, statues and bricked walkways. The State Capitol Building is at one end of the rectangular park, and the City and County Building (*above*) rises at the other end. Additional attractions adjacent to the park include the new Denver Central Public Library, the Denver Art Museum, the Colorado History Museum, a Greek amphitheater and the Webb Municipal Office Building.

Wintertime (*above*)

On a winter day, the Mile-High City settles down beneath a blanket of snow. Being so close to the Front Range of the Rocky Mountains, Denver is often shielded from the heavy snowfalls that occur in the mountains and the prairie regions to the east.

Martin Luther King Memorial (*opposite*)

A provocative memorial in City Park depicts Dr. Martin Luther King delivering his famous *I Have a Dream* speech. Other civil rights leaders are also honored as part of the monument, including Rosa Parks, Frederick Douglass, Soujourner Truth and Mahatma Gandhi.

Cheesman Park Pavilion (*pages 12–13*)

The stately Greek pavilion at Cheesman Park is a popular gathering place for residents of Denver's historic Capitol Hill neighborhood and the site of summer concerts.

Dr. Martin Luther King, Jr.
January 15, 1929 – April 4, 1968

"I Have A Dream"

Nobel Peace Prize
1964

QUIET
RESPECT
PLEASE

Denver Performing Arts Complex *(above)*

This highly acclaimed Performing Arts Complex is the second largest performing arts facility in the world after New York's Lincoln Center. It is home to ten performance spaces totaling over 10,000 seats, all connected by an 80-foot-tall glass atrium.

Dancers *(opposite)*

Dancers, Jonathan Borofsky's stunning sixty-foot-tall steel and fiberglass work, creates a joyful performance atmosphere. It is located on the front lawn of the Denver Performing Arts Complex, also referred to as the DPAC. The internationally acclaimed sculptor also created and recorded *Let's Dance,* the accompanying melody that plays at the site continuously. The playful sculpture is softly lit each evening as the figures dance into the night.

Infinite Energy at the Atrium *(opposite)*

Infinite Energy, by renowned Mexican sculptor Victor M. Contreras, graces the atrium of the Denver Performing Arts Center. The atrium creates an elegant and stimulating entrance to each of ten performance halls that host ballet, opera, theatre and concerts.

The Colorado Convention Center *(above)*

Expanded and renovated in 2004, the Colorado Convention Center, in downtown Denver, features 584,000 square feet of state-of-the-art exhibit halls, ballrooms, an auditorium, and spectacular lobbies on each side with dramatic views of the Rockies as well as the city center.

17

Life in the Tropics

The Boettcher Memorial Tropical Conservatory, the Denver Botanic Gardens' signature building, showcases over one-thousand exotic plants from tropical forests around the world, including a two-story model of a banyan tree, complete with staircase. This conservatory is also famous for its architecture. When it was built in 1966, it was considered to be the first truly modern building in Denver and achieved landmark status just seven years later.

Denver Botanic Gardens *(top and bottom)*

One of the top ten botanical gardens in the West, Denver Botanic Gardens was one of the first in the country to highlight native plants and promote water conservation and natural control of pests. This lush, green oasis opened in 1959. Since then, these gardens have expanded to include a wildlife and native plant refuge in nearby Chatfield, a trail on Mount Evans, and a formal, five-acre garden in downtown Denver.

19

Wellington Webb Municipal Building
(above and opposite)

Built in 2002, this award-winning building was named after Denver's first African-American mayor. The plaza's granite mythical Janus Head sculpture, entitled *East 2 West Source Point*, inspires all to look to the past as well as to the future. At the center, a golden plumb bob symbolizes the location as the origin of "where a city is built." Inside, the artistic theme continues with Larry Kirkland's *Civic Source Point*, a dramatic piece suspended in the lobby's atrium.

Pepsi Center

The Pepsi Center, home to the NBA's Denver
Nuggets and the NHL's Colorado Avalanche, is
part of a six-year plan to upgrade Denver's professional sports venues, including Invesco Field
at Mile High, home to the NFL's Bronco's and
Coors Field, home to MLB's Colorado Rockies.

The Broncos

On the south side of the Denver Broncos' new
football stadium, seven larger-than-life horses
run uphill alongside a raging stream in a
rugged, rocky mountain setting. *The Broncos*
was designed by famed Italian sculptor, Sergio
Benvenuti.

Invesco Field at Mile High *(top)*

The Denver Broncos play in front of wildly enthusiastic fans at their new, high-tech stadium, Invesco Field. One of the league's top franchises, the Broncos have gone to the Super Bowl six times and won back to back championships in 1998 and 1999.

A Grand Entrance *(bottom)*

Illuminated sculptures decorate the grounds of the new, 20,000-seat Pepsi Center arena, home to the NBA Denver Nuggets, NHL Colorado Avalanche and AFL Colorado Crush. Between games, the facility hosts big-name concerts.

Home of the Colorado Rockies *(opposite)*

Fireworks light up the night skies at Coors Field, the Rockies' new ballpark. Dedicated Denver sports fans have led the National League in attendance.

Memorial Day Parade *(above)*

Members of the Ford Model-T Automobile Club show off their antique cars in Denver's annual Memorial Day parade. The procession honors veterans of American wars from the Civil War to the current war in Iraq.

Tabor Center *(opposite)*

Part of the fashionable 16th Street Mall, Tabor Center, along with the Westin Tabor building next door, renovated and expanded their shopping mall area and added ESPN Zone, a unique 23,000-square-foot sports restaurant and store.

Catch a Free Ride *(above)*

Ranked the number one metro tourist attraction,
Denver's 16th Street Mall is a 16-block-long
pedestrian and transitway concourse in the
center of downtown. More than 60,000 people
board the location's free shuttle buses on week-
days.

Mile High Center *(opposite)*

This distinctive *cash register* shaped building is
officially known as 1700 Broadway and is part
of a complex that includes the Wells Fargo
Center. One of his first high-rise commissions,
the Mile High Center was designed by the
esteemed architect I.M. Pei.

City Beautiful (*top*)

One of six sculptures on a freeway viaduct into downtown Denver, this fabricated steel piece by local artist David Griggs, entitled, *Platte Valley Time Vanes*, honors the visionary *City Beautiful* program of Robert W. Speer, one of Denver's most influential mayors.

Big Wheel (*bottom*)

Atop the city's pump house, the monumental sculpture, *Big Wheel*, by artist Ed Carpenter, celebrates the city's transportation and manufacturing industries.

A Treasure at the Rainbow's End *(above)*

A fiery rainbow streaks across the Denver sky.
With a metro area of 2.6 million people, the
Mile-High City is the cultural, financial and
entertainment hub of a region that spans six-
hundred miles in any direction.

Just Before Dawn *(pages 32–33)*

Downtown's skyscrapers pierce the Mile-
High City dawn following an exciting night
enjoying performances, clubs and restaurants.
Sunshine greets joggers, bakers, and other
early risers an average of 310 days per year
in Denver.

Denver Sunrise *(top)*

The first light of day blankets the city in a golden glow against the distant Rocky Mountains. Situated exactly one mile above sea level, Denver enjoys fresh, crisp air and a mountain panorama of nearly two-hundred peaks.

End of the Day *(bottom)*

Union Station's vintage neon sign glows in the fading light of dusk while downtown businesses wrap it up for the day and commuters head home. Denver has the tenth largest downtown in the country and a bustling, mile-long pedestrian mall.

Sloan's Lake *(opposite)*

In 1861, farmer Thomas Sloan dug a well and woke up the next morning to a growing lake on his property. Today, Sloan's Lake Park is a popular destination for Denverites who relax on the grass, or take to the lake for water sports.

Sunset at Sloan's Lake Park *(top)*

Clouds stretch far and wide over Denver's
Sloan's Lake Park. The two-hundred-acre park,
with its glassy-smooth lake, running path, and
playground, is perfect for exercise, picnicking,
boating or fishing from the shore.

Foothills of the Rockies *(bottom)*

The foothills of the Rockies are poised at
Denver's western doorstep, offering an expan-
sive network of trails that beckon hikers of all
skill levels. In contrast, to the east lies a level
and arid plain made green mostly by irrigation
and planting.

Mount Evans (*above*)

Denver is blessed with one of the most spectacular geographical settings in the world. At her back door are the rolling foothills of the Rockies and the magnificent, snow-capped Mount Evans (14,264 feet), one of the tallest mountains in the Front Range.

Inspiration Point Park (*pages 38–39*)

Northwest of the city, towards Boulder, is a picture-postcard view of the famous Flatirons. These giant slabs of tilted rock are the ancestors of the forces that formed the present Rocky Mountain Range.

City Park Golf Course *(top)*

This 18-hole regulation golf course in Denver's premier city park has a new, spacious club house, pro shop, and restaurant, and offers a challenging new water hazard to golfers. The course runs adjacent to the Denver Zoo and Denver Museum of Nature and Science.

City Park Pavilion *(bottom)*

Designed in 1886 by architects John Humphreys and William Fisher, City Park Pavilion is a Spanish-style, architectural treasure on Ferril Lake. Now a renovated historic site, this beautiful landmark hosts many public and private events.

Ferril Lake *(opposite)*

A gaggle of geese paddles along the tranquil waters of Ferril Lake, one of two lakes at City Park. The lake can be explored from a rented paddleboat, or along one of the many serene walking paths throughout this urban oasis.

Premiere Biking Paths

More than 130 miles of bike paths connect through Denver's 205 parks and the foothills beyond, providing scenic rides with a spectacular Rocky Mountain backdrop. Above, three cyclists pedal along a Cherry Creek path in Confluence Park, while, opposite, a landscaped pathway meanders along the peaceful water in Sloan's Lake Park. *Bicycle Magazine* has named Denver the nation's top city for bicycling.

The Cyclone *(top)*

Built in 1940, Lakeside Amusement Park's wooden roller coaster, The Cyclone, is still in operation today. To its left is the tower of the old Lakeside ballroom where big-name bands once echoed across Berkeley Lake.

Denver Skate Park *(bottom)*

Denver Skate Park is a well-designed skateboard venue with a wide variety of challenging features, from warm-up moguls to deep bowls, including one that measures twelve feet deep with a ladder for climbing out. It also has a shaded picnic area and night lighting.

Defying Gravity *(opposite)*

A seasoned skateboarder rides the rim of a deep bowl at Denver Skate Park, the largest skateboarding park in Colorado. In addition to bowls and moguls, this top-notch park includes street terrain and stair venues.

Wakeboarding *(top)*

Riding a wake-board is just part of the fun awaiting Denverites on a hot, summer day at beautiful Sloan's Lake. Fishermen also come to this well-stocked lake to catch bullhead, catfish and rainbow trout.

Kayaking at Confluence Park *(bottom)*

Denver's Confluence Park, on the nexus of Cherry Creek and the South Platte River, is well-known among kayakers as the location of some of the river's premier kayak chutes. It's a beautiful and convenient place to practice white-water skills.

Ballooning *(opposite)*

Denver averages over 300 sunny days each year which makes it a perfect place for hot air balloon rides. Timeless and romantic, floating along in a billowing balloon from southwest Denver's Chatfield State Park, is a spectacular way to see the Rockies.

Articulated Wall (*opposite*)

This massive 85-foot-tall sculpture by Herbert Bayer is the colorful twisting landmark of the Denver Design District, the city's wholesale showrooms for interior designers, architects, and builders. More than eighteen-hundred different design lines are displayed.

Sidewalk Art at Larimer Square (*top*)

The award-winning Comcast La Piazza dell' Arte festival celebrates the street painting traditions of 16th-century Renaissance Italy. During that time, artists created chalk paintings of the Madonna. Today, this festival's chalk art has a freer and more stylized approach.

Fish for Dinner (*bottom*)

The newly re-designed Downtown Aquarium blends dining and entertainment with underwater exhibits in a one million gallon aquarium. Fish, sharks, and stingrays swim by the dining tables at the Aquarium Restaurant.

Moo-ving Sculptures

Throughout Denver, brightly decorated cows created by local artists playfully roam city sidewalks. In 2006, the much-anticipated Denver Cow Parade culminated in a cow auction that raised money for local non-profit organizations.

Platte River Bike Path

Colorful tile, brick and clay murals that comprise the work, *A Life in Harmony with All Creation,* by Maria Alquilar, and Ken and Judith Williams, vibrantly enhance the pathway along the Platte River at the 15th Street Viaduct.

Six Flags Elitch Gardens (top)

Denver has two wonderful theme parks—
Lakeside Amusement Park, an historic amusement park on Lake Rhoda and the newer Six
Flags Elitch Gardens that features fifty rides,
along with entertaining shows and attractions
guaranteed to please.

Denver Diner (bottom)

The popular, neon-lit Denver Diner seems
oblivious to the modern city that surrounds it,
and is more reminiscent of the post-WW II
days of the restless *Beat Generation*, an attitude
defined by beat poet Jack Kerouac and
Denverite Neal Cassady.

Vintage Trolley Tour (top)

A vintage trolley ride is a great way to enjoy the many sites along the South Platte River, Confluence Park, Downtown Aquarium, the Children's Museum and the Denver Broncos' Invesco Field at Mile High. The Six Flags Elitch Gardens' rollercoaster rises from behind.

The Mind Eraser at Elitch Gardens (bottom)

The granddaddy of all roller coasters, this world-class monster, suspension thrill-ride, soars over ten stories skyward, then plummets down at speeds topping sixty miles an hour.

Denver Art Museum *(top)*

The Denver Art Museum's exceptional collection of Native American art begins outdoors with *Wheel*, by Yoruba artist Edgar Heap of Birds. Inspired by the Big Horn medicine wheel, ten tree forms are aligned with the summer solstice.

Big Sweep *(bottom)*

How do you tackle big, cleaning jobs? With this whimsical, 35-foot broom and dust pan by famed sculptors Oldenburg and van Bruggen. Positioned outside the Denver Art Museum's Hamilton Building, *Big Sweep* is a preview of the diverse art collection inside.

Lao Tzu Sculpture *(opposite)*

Erected in 1996 in the Acoma Plaza, *Lao Tzu*, by award-winning sculptor Mark di Suvero, is a 30-foot-tall, 16-ton abstract wonder. The bright orange structure made from industrial I-beams, is named for Chinese philosopher, Lao Tzu.

Children's Museum *(top)*

Originally set up in an old school bus, the Children's Museum of Denver expanded to this spacious, crayon-colored facility. It offers inter-active learning playscapes for newborns to age eight as well as their grown-ups.

Colorado History Museum *(above)*

Explore Colorado's history from prehistoric times to the recent past via historic artifacts and state-of-the-art exhibits. The mural along the museum's entrance wall is a combination of 15 different works of art associated with the 12 sites run by the Colorado Historical Society.

The Denver Zoo *(opposite)*

Home to nearly 4,000 animals from seven-hundred species, the Denver Zoo is also famous for its collection of exquisite animal sculptures. Artist Heath Satow created twenty two life-size sculptures of giraffes and other animals for the zoo's plaza.

Denver Museum of Nature and Science
(top and opposite)

The Denver Museum of Nature and Science is the top museum of its kind in the Rocky Mountain region. It has an impressive collection of dinosaur skeletons along with plant and animal fossils. From ancient Egypt to the farthest reaches of outer space with its terrific *Space Odyssey* exhibit, the museum offers an incredible experience with the natural wonders in our backyards, the world, and beyond.

Museo de Las Americas *(bottom)*

The Museo de Las Americas is in step with Denver's growing Latino population. With over 4,000 objects, its two main collections focus on *Ancient Art of the Americas* and the more contemporary *Art of the People*.

Shorter Community A.M.E. Church

The first African-American church established in Colorado, this historic building is now home to the accomplished African American, *Cleo Parker Robinson Dance Troupe.* The dance company's founder and namesake has earned respect for her leadership role in the Denver community, and high praise in the national dance circuit for her outstanding choreography and the ensemble's performances.

Kirkland Museum (top)

The Kirkland Museum was created to house the artwork of Vance Kirkland, the founding director of the Art School at the University of Denver. The museum is internationally recognized for its 20th-century decorative arts collection.

Denver Museum of Miniatures, Dolls and Toys (bottom)

This international collection of children's toys, antique dolls and playhouses reveals many aspects of history, fashion, art, architecture and lifestyles from the 16th century to modern times.

Fire Station No. 3

In 1893, Denver's segregated Second District,
was one of the first to have an all African-
American Fire Company. Integrated into the
entire DFD since 1958, Station No. 3 is one
of thirty-four active stations serving Denver.

Forney Transportation Museum (*top*)

The one-of-a-kind collection at the Forney Transportation Museum features antique cars, an 1811 stagecoach, Prince Aly Kahn's Rolls Royce, Amelia Earhardt's "Gold Bug" Kissel, and the Forney locomotive used on elevated tracks in New York and Chicago.

Denver Firefighters Museum (*bottom*)

Located in Denver's historic Fire Station No. 1, the Firefighters Museum teaches fire prevention while displaying the proud history of Denver's fire department. Visitors can try on firefighting equipment, slide down a pole and ride on a firetruck.

Fillmore Auditorium (*top*)

Built in 1907 as a skating rink, the historic Fillmore Auditorium became Mammoth Gardens in 1969, hosting bands like The Who and The Grateful Dead before closing in 1979. It reopened in 1990, and was renamed Fillmore Auditorium in 1999.

Ellie Caulkins Opera House (*bottom*)

Built in 1908, the Municipal Auditorium is the oldest section of the DPAC. It was rededicated as The Quigg Newton Denver Municipal Auditorium in 2002 and underwent a major renovation in 2005. The auditorium is now home to the Ellie Caulkins Opera House.

The Mayan Theatre (*opposite*)

Located in the Baker District, the celebrated Mayan Theatre, built in 1930, is one of the country's three remaining theatres designed in the Art Deco Mayan Revival style. Restored to full glory, the Mayan features independent and foreign language films.

MAYAN

ASK ABOUT
OUR THEATRE RENTALS
GROUP RATES AVAILABLE

THANK U FOR SMOKING
DEVIL&DANIEL JOHNSTON
DONT COME KNOCKING

BREW&VIEW
IN THE MAYAN
FULL BAR UPSTAIRS

BROADWAY
PARTNERSHIP
MDLDC

Denver Victorian Playhouse *(top)*

At the turn of the 20th century, George Swartz, a Shakespearean virtuoso suffering from tuberculosis, moved to the dry, sunny climate of Denver. He built a house and established the Bungalow Theater in his basement where he would eventually produce all of the Great Bard's plays. With a more eclectic repertoire, the tradition continues today in its unique setting.

Confluence Jazz Festival *(bottom)*

Every summer, Confluence Park hosts a free *Smooth Jazz* series. The hillside setting makes for excellent acoustics, while the surrounding scenery, warm summer sun, along with a pleasant melody, are a treat for the senses.

The Colorado Symphony

The Colorado Symphony Orchestra performs
under the stars at Cheesman Park during the
free summer park concert series. The orchestra
can also be seen regularly at the beautiful
Boettcher Concert Hall in the Denver Performing Arts Complex.

Fiesta Colorado Dancers *(top)*

As part of Denver's City Free Concert Series held at various parks and locations around the metropolitan area, this Hispanic dance troupe performs for lunchtime crowds at Skyline Park on the 16th Street Mall.

Denver Black Arts Festival *(bottom)*

The popular Denver Black Arts Festival attracts over 100,000 people every summer with arts and crafts exhibits, theater, live performances of dance and music, including jazz, gospel, blues, hip-hop, rock 'n roll and traditional African music.

Cinco de Mayo *(opposite)*

Althought this festival had humble beginnings, the Cinco de Mayo festival now draws more than a million people for one of the largest cultural events in the city. Parades, fabulous food and music, along with children's attractions, make it a perfect family event.

The Oxford Hotel *(top)*

For over a hundred years, The Oxford Hotel, in the Lower Downtown Historical District, has claimed, *"Through these arches, is the hub of Denver."* Reopened, after a $12 million restoration in 1983, it is once again, *"One of the 50 most romantic hotels in the world."*

Larimer Square *(bottom)*

The LoDo District was created by a city council initiative that saved the area's 127 remaining historic structures from the wrecking ball. The result is revitalized residential areas and a charming district that includes the colorful awnings and elegant shops of Larimer Square.

Byron White Courthouse

Erected between 1910 and 1916 as the Federal
Courthouse and Post Office, renovations in the
early 1990's returned the building's marble inte-
riors to its original Renaissance Revival grandeur.
Abundant natural light is evident in its massive
skylights and interior courtyard.

Mountain States Telephone and Telegraph Company Headquarters

The outer lobby of 931 Fourteenth Street in Colorado's Bell System Palace pays homage to the history of communications in the West with four Art Deco murals (1929) by Colorado artist, Allen Tupper True, including this one, entitled *City Telephone Construction.* The site is now on the National Register of Historic Places.

LoDo Ice House

The Ice House, with its intricate masonry design, was a turn-of-the-century creamery and cold storage warehouse. Added to the National Register of Historic Places in 1985, the building now serves as trendy lofts. It is located next to Union Station in the LoDo District.

Blair Caldwell African American Research Library *(above)*

A division of the Denver Public Library, this new specialty library is the gateway to the Welton Street Historic District. The building entrance is flanked by the striking bronze and mosaic reliefs of an African American man and woman. Created by internationally renowned artist Thomas Jay Warren, the evocative reliefs reflect the noble strength and pioneer spirit of the early American West's African Americans.

Black American West Museum *(opposite)*

The Black American West Museum focuses on the substantial contributions by African Americans toward the development of the American West. Plaques in the walkway pay tribute to some of the West's first black cowboys.

GOSSIP
Martha Pettigrew ~ Sculptor

THE KNOX GALLERIES
www.knoxgalleries.com

Gossip *(opposite)*

This delightful sculpture in Writer Square depicts barefoot washerwomen, with baskets of laundry, leaning on a wall while conversing, undoubtedly, over some juicy gossip. Denver is well known for its eclectic variety of acclaimed public art.

Denver Central Public Library *(top)*

Designed by world-famous architect, Michael Graves, the legendary co-founder of the post-modern school of architecture, the Denver Central Public Library is the largest library between Los Angeles and Chicago, welcoming one million people annually.

Writer Square *(bottom)*

The updated Writer Square near the 16th Street Mall and adjacent to the LoDo District, offers high-end shops and galleries to visit and restaurants and cafés to enjoy.

Holiday Time (*opposite*)

The season is bright with the festive lights of the 16th Street Mall plaza. The iconic D&F Tower was part of the Daniels & Fisher Department Store in 1910. Modeled after the St. Mark's Bell Tower in Venice, today its basement hosts a popular cabaret.

Denver Gas and Electric Building (*above*)

The Denver Gas and Electric building has a running start on all others when it comes to holiday decorating. Built in 1910, its façade includes a unique flared cornice above arched top story windows and is illuminated with 13,000 electric lights year-round.

Ringing in the New Year (*opposite*)

Approximately 200,000 people will welcome in the new year as fireworks explode over the 16th Street Mall. Two identical, heart-stopping fireworks displays are set off at both nine and midnight for the optimum holiday effect.

National Western Stock Show (*top and bottom*)

With its debut in 1906, this "Super Bowl" of livestock shows continues to be the largest of its kind in the world. One hundred years later, at the 2006 event, the Horse Show segment alone recorded more than 18,000 entries, while the Cattle Show exhibited twenty breeds and the Rodeo Show had enough nonstop spills and thrills to earn it the Professional Rodeo Cowboys Association's title of "Indoor Rodeo of the Year."

Union Station Lights Up

Throughout the holidays, a grand illumination occurs in and around Denver's downtown area. At dusk, the Mile-High City slowly turns into a painted canvas. Denver's Union Station is decorated with more than 100 floodlights, creating a beacon of light at the end of 17th Street.

Colorful Holiday Cheer

A rainbow of colors herald in the holiday season at the Denver City and County Courthouse. The ornate light show is a bright part of the Denver holiday festivities that include two fantastic fireworks displays.

Denver International Airport *(top and bottom)*

Denver International Airport's unique tension fabric roof design mimics the snow-capped Rockies that surround it. As part of Denver's "Art in Public Places" initiative, artists integrated actual structural art, murals and sculptures into the design and systems of the building. The world's second largest airport and one of the ten busiest, the DIA's state-of-the-art facility offers public Wi-Fi access for travelers with laptops. The fusion of art and architecture, as well as cutting edge technology, makes DIA truly remarkable among the nation's airports.

Regis University

Regis University is comprised of three colleges: Regis College, the Rueckert-Hartman School for Health Professions and the School for Professional Studies. It has been named one of the best universities in the country for eleven years, by *U.S. News & World Report*.

Tivoli Student Union

One of the most successful breweries in the Rockies until its closing in 1966, the Tivoli building was named after the famed Tivoli Gardens in Denmark. The flamboyant national historic landmark was restored and reopened in 1994 as a combination retail center and student union for the Auraria Higher Education Center. The center is shared by the students of Denver's three non-resident schools: the Community College of Denver, the Metropolitan State College of Denver and the University of Colorado at Denver.

St. Cajetan's Center (*top*)

In 1925, this lovely Spanish Colonial church was built to service Auraria's Spanish residents. When the Auraria Campus was built in 1973, the parish re-located and the historic church became a multi-purpose auditorium for the community.

Knight-Wood House (*bottom*)

The 1920's Knight-Wood House, located on the Auraria Campus, is an excellent example of Craftsman-style architecture, a response to increasing industrialization in America. The detailed style showcased the fine construction details of traditional artisans.

Denver University *(top and bottom)*

Five-hundred-million dollars in capital improvements have enhanced Denver University in the last decade. Its flagships are the new law school, with personal computer amenities for each student, and the acclaimed Newman Center for the Performing Arts. The Newman Center facilities include a four-level opera house, a new theatre space for resident thespians, and a new recital hall.

Denver University Law School *(opposite)*

When The Sturm College of Law opened in 1892, its presence and resources helped to establish relevant laws for the Colorado area frontier, taking some of the *wild* out of the "Wild West." Today, Sturm Law graduates are in demand throughout the United States.

Historic Temple Emanuel *(top)*

Adorned with two copper topped minarets, the original 1899 Jewish temple reflects a Byzantine/Moorish architectural style. Today, it is an events center for concerts, performing arts, meetings and weddings.

New Life *(bottom)*

Originally home to a Methodist Episcopal congregation in 1871, the chapel was built with rhyolite stone from Castlewood Canyon and Colorado red sandstone trim. More recently, this suburban sanctuary has been redesigned to house spacious residential lofts.

Cathedral of the Immaculate Conception *(opposite)*

This stunning Gothic-style cathedral, with its 210-foot-tall bell spires, was built using granite and limestone in 1911. Its seventy-five stained glass windows, designed by German master, F.X. Zettler, are world-famous.

Holy Ghost Church (*opposite*)

Begun in 1924, funding for the completion of
the Holy Ghost Church did not come through
until 1940. Three hundred tons of Colorado
colocreme travertine marble grace the walls and
columns of the church, making it the largest
collection of this stone in the United States.

The adjacent 40-story office tower, 1999 Broadway, was built on the site in 1985, providing
the Holy Ghost parish with funds to support
their homeless programs. The integration of
the historic and the modern is truly symbolic
of Denver.

Historic Schleier Mansion (*above*)

This national landmark house was built in the
1880's for a successful local businessman.
Constructed of red sandstone, it is an excellent
example of the Queen Anne style. It features
an onion-domed tower and eight ornate fire-
places inside.

Castle Marne Bed & Breakfast *(top)*

The famous 19th-century architect, William Land, designed this great mansion in 1889, now a charming B&B. The Victorian style is accentuated with balconies, a four-story tower and a stained glass "Peacock Window."

Byers-Evans House Museum *(bottom)*

One of Denver's great historic houses, this elegant 1883 residence was owned by newspaper publisher William Byers and later sold to William Gray Evans. Visitors can see a short film about these movers and shakers.

Capitol Hill Mansion B&B *(opposite)*

Built in 1891, this home was one of the last, private mansions erected in Denver before the Silver Crash of 1893. Now an elegant bed and breakfast, the stone house has eight 19th-century-style rooms.

Clement's Addition *(top)*

The Clement's Addition Historic District is one of Denver's oldest, residential areas. Nineteenth-century Queen Anne homes and row houses occupy the neighborhood, as well as the Zion Baptist Church, established by freed slaves in 1865.

Capitol Hill Historic District *(bottom)*

One of Denver's first wealthy neighborhoods, Capitol Hill has many 19th-century homes and mansions on tree-lined streets. The 16th Street Mall, museums, and other downtown attractions are a short walk away.

Molly Brown House Museum *(opposite)*

"The Unsinkable" Molly Brown's 1886 Capitol Hill home is a lasting symbol of the Victorian era and the lifestyle of those fortunate enough to acquire their wealth in mining, railroads, and commerce in the late 19th century.

Belleview College & Preparatory School (top)

Owned and operated by the Pillar of Fire Church, Belleview College in Westminster consists of an elementary school, high school, junior college and Bible seminary. The main building, Westminster Castle, is a 1908 landmark.

Foothills Art Center (bottom)

The Foothills Art Center in Golden, Colorado includes two buildings on the National Historic Register: Foothills I, the original First Presbyterian Church, built in 1872 and its connected parsonage which houses six galleries, as well as Foothills II, an adjacent historical mansion.

Jealousy (opposite)

Jealousy, by Harry Marinsky, is located at the Museum of Outdoor Arts in Greenwood Plaza. The museum incorporates fine art, architecture and landscape design throughout the grounds and exhibition interior, promoting its theme, "art is a part of everyday life."

Air and Space Museum *(top and bottom)*

Inside the Air and Space Museum, located at
the old Lowry AFB, there are twenty of the
most impressive fighters and bombers the U.S.
has ever produced, including the Stratofortress,
the Star Fighter, and a full-size mockup of a
manned space station crew module.

Jefferson County Government Center

Nicknamed the *Taj Mahal*, the Jefferson County Government Center presides over a county that is predominant in the history of the "Wild, Wild West". In 1858, gold was discovered in the Rockies and the small settlement of Golden (population, 200) exploded with growth, experiencing all the challenges and opportunities that came along with *gold fever*. In addition, Buffalo Bill, various members of the Hole-in-the-Wall Gang, and other notables made headlines in the local newspapers with their bold crimes or heroic adventures.

Lakewood Cultural Center

Created as a community arts resource center,
the Lakewood Cultural Center's 310-seat
theater, classrooms, and gallery space support
local events and presentations, visual arts
exhibits, and live performances, as well as a
variety of instructional programs.

Lakewood Heritage Visitors Center

Lakewood Heritage Visitors Center chronicles the history of Denver through walking tours of notable buildings, cultural enrichment programs, and a history book club. For crafts lovers, the center also offers classes in quilting and rug hooking.

Lakewood Heritage Center *(top)*

Lakewood Heritage Center in Belmar Park includes architecture that showcases life in Colorado at the turn of the 20th century, with barns, farm houses, an old country school, a pump house and a water tower.

Clear Creek History Park *(bottom)*

This hands-on park provides work and play activities like those of settlers in the late 1800's, including lasso throwing, gold panning, wool spinning, blacksmithing, and a live schoolhouse class. The "M" on Lookout Mountain in the background, represents, "The School of Mines".

Argo Gold Mine and Mill Museum *(opposite)*

The Mighty Argo, in Idaho Springs, was the most sophisticated of its day and the largest gold ore milling operation in the world, processing over $200 million dollars of ore over a fifty-year period.

Astor House Museum

A national landmark in Golden, Colorado, the 1867 Astor House is restored to its original glory as a late Victorian western hotel and boarding house. As a boarding house, it was a popular residence for students at the Colorado School of Mines.

The Colorado School of Mines

The Colorado School of Mines is a public research university located in Golden, specializing in engineering, applied science and geophysics. The university is renowned for its extensive curriculum and research program that focuses on responsible stewardship of the earth's resources. It is one of very few in the world that has a broad expertise in resource exploration, extraction, production and utilization. CSM has the highest admission standards of any public state university in Colorado.

Wildlife Experience *(top, left and opposite)*

The Wildlife Experience, in the city of Parker, offers films and extensive exhibits of art work and interactive programs on local geology, ecosystems, plants and animals, in addition to a gallery on the grasslands of Africa.

Water World *(above and left)*

Denver's Water World has been wet for twenty-five years, and it's getting wetter, with miles of slides, four million gallons of water, and heart-pumping drops. The word going around is that "Journey to the Center of the Earth" and the "Zoomerang" are *way cool*.

Renaissance Fair *(top and bottom)*

The immensely popular Renaissance Festival, in Larkspur, Colorado, replicates a 16th-century English country village. Armored knights at jousting tournaments and 250 shops with wares, highlight the charm of this 30-year tradition.

Mount Evans Landscape *(pages 112–113)*

The Mount Evans Scenic Byway leads to the top of the 14,264-foot mountain. Sure-footed mountain goats with their short, straight horns and white goatees, can be found throughout the Wilderness Area of Mount Evans.

Red Rocks Park, Morrison *(top and bottom)*

Red Rocks Park is known for its massive, red sandstone boulders. The famous formation, Ship Rock, is shaped like a vessel and is balanced on another boulder so precariously that it rocks back and forth when the wind blows.

Red Rocks Amphitheater *(opposite)*

Flanked by two 300-foot-tall red rocks, this amphitheater is a natural geological creation, providing perfect acoustics and a scenic backdrop for summer concerts. With a formal stage and seating created in 1941, it accommodates nearly 10,000 people.

Garden of the Gods Park *(116–117)*

Most of the 488 acres that make up the awe-inspiring "Garden of the Gods", was owned by the Burlington Railroad's Perkins family who, in 1909, donated it to the city of Colorado Springs for the public to enjoy. Narrated tours of the park are offered at the Visitors Center.

Genesee, Colorado *(above)*

Just sixteen miles outside of Denver, Genesee is a community of 3,500 residents that offers the tranquility and beauty of mountain living. With over 1,000 acres of protected open space, the area defines "the great outdoors".

Cherry Creek Trail *(opposite)*

This is a favorite trail with bicyclists and other locals because it follows Cherry Creek all the way from Cherry Creek Reservoir to the middle of downtown Denver. It connects with some of the 800 miles of bike paths that surround Denver.

Paragliding

Paragliding offers contemporary pioneers a tranquil birds-eye view of some of the most breathtaking scenery in the country. Lookout Mountain has several outstanding take-off points where adverturers can undertake the ultimate in this exciting experience.

Standley Lake, Westminster

Standley Lake is a favorite boating and fishing lake and a city reservoir. A protected, natural grassland prairie stretches for miles on its north and south shores, creating a natural buffer between residential areas and the lake. When the winds sweep down from the mountains, the otherwise tranquil lake is stirred up with frothy whitecaps. Visitors enjoy picnicking, walking the lakeside trails, and taking in the panoramic views of the Indian Peaks Wilderness Area and the Flatirons.

Kayaking Clear Creek *(left)*

The city of Golden has a unique, whitewater kayaking park on Clear Creek for different skill levels. Built with natural boulders that create plenty of whitewater, the bottom of the 800-foot course demands every skill you have.

Climbing the Wall *(right)*

Sheer canyon walls rise up several hundred feet while Clear Creek rushes below and echoes off the canyon walls. This is a rock climbing mecca with areas that will challenge even the best climbers, like, "Head Like a Hole", in "Pete's Wicked Cave" or "The Monastery."

Lariat Loop Scenic Byway

Meandering bike paths of downtown Denver give way to more challenging terrain to the west, traveling up Lookout Mountain to the grave site of Buffalo Bill and the nature center. World-class cyclists come to this area for the demanding training and the sheer beauty.

Eldorado Canyon State Park

Eldorado Canyon State Park is "where the canyon meets the sky." The park boasts five-hundred technical rock climbing routes for experts and eleven miles of scenic hiking and mountain biking trails. Though this outdoor wonderland can demand great physical endurance and prowess, those who prefer less rigorous activity are also rewarded with nature's immense quiet and beauty.

An Autumn Snowfall

An October snowfall dusts the Flatirons, north of Eldorado Canyon, but leaves the scarlet sumac foliage at their base untouched. Climbing without the use of ropes on large rock formations, or *bouldering*, is popular all along the Front Range. The Ghetto, Satellite Boulders, and Terrain Boulders are sites known for such climbing on the Flatirons, but please remember: leave no bolts and climbing is closed from February through July while resident raptors are nesting.

Vail Ski Resort *(opposite)*

Vail is the recognized "king" of ski resorts with its charming village setting of boutiques and restaurants. Over five-thousand acres of world-class skiing easily qualify Vail as "The Switzerland of the Americas."

Breckenridge *(top and bottom)*

The premiere wintertime attraction of this 147-year-old Victorian town is its amazing variety of world-class ski slopes that cater to all skill levels. As the largest historic district in Colorado, the Town of Breckenridge has plenty to explore.

127

John Kieffer

Photographer John Kieffer's first visit to the Mile-High city was nearly 40 years ago, and he immediately sensed Colorado would become his home. Having worked in and photographed the Denver area since college, when approached about creating a photographic portrait of Denver, John jumped at the chance to show what this diverse and friendly city has to offer.

Based in Boulder, John Kieffer has had a varied career as a professional photographer and writer shooting projects that range from renowned nature and recreation publications to advertising. Other books by John Kieffer include: *The Photographer's Assistant, Mastering Nature Photography,* and *Boulder, Colorado: A Photographic Portrait.*

www.KiefferNatureStock.com